Take God at His Word
Experience the Power of Giving

by Dr. Kregg Hood

Take God at His Word
Experience the Power of Giving
ISBN 0-9764278-4-2
Copyright © 2009 Dr. Kregg Hood
For more information, contact:
Dr. Kregg Hood
1428 N. Rich Hill Circle
Nixa, MO 65714
(940) 300-8498
Kregghood.com

CONTENTS

How to Get the Most from
Take God at His Word

You're about to begin an exciting journey through God's Word. Prepare to allow His principles and plans to transform your perceptions about giving. As you do, the Lord will revolutionize your understanding of His goodness and faithfulness. Since the Lord already owns everything, He doesn't need anything to be given to Him. Instead, as Jesus put it, *"but seek first his kingdom and his righteousness, and all these things will be given to you as well"* (Matthew 6:33). This means giving will open doors of blessing to us! We can reject the Enemy's efforts to trap us with guilt and fear because we are learning to truly take God at His Word.

Follow these guidelines faithfully, and you'll discover how exciting, joyful, and empowering giving to God can be.

1. Read one chapter each week. It's usually best to take time on Monday or Tuesday since you will have more time to read and process these insights. If you have a family, take turns reading the chapter out loud together.

2. Discuss the principles with close friends or family members. If you have children living at home, include them too. It's especially valuable to meet "around the kitchen table" at least one evening each week. The questions at the end of each chapter help you see God as the source of your blessings. Talk and pray together

about your experiences with money and giving. Discuss parents' influence too. If married, note the areas in which you and your mate agree, as well as where you disagree. Continue to talk and pray about the points on which you disagree until God leads you to a place of unity.

3. Pray for God's wisdom regarding financial matters. Allow the Lord to speak to you about your needs, spending, giving, and overall financial attitudes and habits. Ask Him to guard your heart from fear and lead you to trust Him with your giving decisions. Give Him every fear and ask for supernatural wisdom and strength.

We've now started on a new journey of faith. May the Lord bless you in more ways than you can ask or imagine (Ephesians 3:20).

Dr. Kregg Hood
Springfield, Missouri

2 Corinthians 9:10,11

Now he who supplies seed to the sower and bread for food will also supply and increase your store of seed and will enlarge the harvest of your righteousness. You will be made rich in every way so that you can be generous on every occasion, and through us your generosity will result in thanksgiving to God.

In the next few pages, you'll discover:

- ❖ God is the Source of your financial blessings.

- ❖ God gives financial rewards when you take Him at His Word with your giving.

- ❖ The more you give, the more you will receive.

WORD ONE
I Will Make You Rich in Every Way

Years ago, a man was building a house in rural New England. Needing water for his new home, he commissioned an expert to dig a well for him. The old well digger, seasoned in the art of his trade, scouted out the property, searching for the right spot to sink a shaft. Sure enough, he found an underground river and put in a well.

Packing up his gear to leave, he left the homeowner with some important advice: "Every day you must pump some water from the well. If you don't, you'll be sorry." The homeowner thanked the man for the advice, and for weeks he followed the well digger's counsel and pumped water every day.

As time went on, the homeowner began to take the cool, sweet water for granted. One day he left on a trip and forgot to get someone to pump water for him each day while he was away. When he returned, the water at the bottom of the well was stagnant and almost gone. He tried pumping in fresh water, but nothing came out.

Later, he went to town and told the well digger his well had dried up. The old gentleman asked, "Did you remember to pump water from the well every day?" The younger man confessed his neglect and asked why this mattered. The well digger replied, "The water in the well comes from an underground river that feeds the small tributaries of water which are connected to your well. Water must continue to flow through these small tributaries so that the well can receive water. If you quit pumping the water, the ground will dry up slightly and the underground river can't find its way to your well. This cuts off the water supply."

Then the old man concluded, "Remember, the source of the water is the river, not the well."[1]

If the source of your financial strength is your own personal well of resources, you risk running dry!

The Difference Between Source and Means

Recognizing the difference between source and means can be tough. Our bank accounts, our abilities, and our intellects are not the sources of our provision and blessings. They are simply the means by which God, the Source, provides blessing. God provides for our needs according to His riches. He uses the material resources of our world as the delivery system to care for His children. To experience His abundance, we must first see Him as the Source of every blessing.

Secondly, we must take Him at His Word because we trust that His Word is true. Spiritual principles about giving relate closely to how God chooses either to bless us or to withhold His blessing. If we want our wells to contain enough resources to function effectively in our world, we must trust God and follow His teachings. The Bible teaches that giving generously out of love for God will tap you into God's unseen river of blessing.

God Will Be the Source of Your Blessing

We will improve our attitudes about giving when we recognize that God will be the Source of our blessings. In Paul's thank-you note to the church at Philippi for their financial support, he says, "And my God will meet all your needs according to his glorious riches in Christ Jesus" (Philippians 4:19). Paul said that God would meet every need they had. That is an awesome promise to Christians!

God's Law of the Harvest

The way we share our resources may be the most practical issue we face. Every successful farmer knows that he must sow seed if he wants to reap a crop. Scripture clearly teaches this concept. It is often referred to as the "law of the harvest." Simply stated, the more you want to reap, the more you have to sow.

My good friend and co-worker, Roger Lane, has a farming background. Recently, he shared a fascinating illustration on how farmers plan when they want to have a good crop. You'll see the obvious connection to giving too. Roger said that if you want to have a good harvest it is essential that you have a good stand (healthy plants) approximately 8 inches apart in 30-inch rows. This means that you will have to plant approximately 30,000 to 32,000 seeds per acre. If you sow sparingly you will not have a good stand. You must sow bountifully if you want to reap or harvest bountifully.

This principle is first found in Genesis 8:22: "As long as the earth endures, seedtime and harvest, cold and heat, summer and winter, day and night will never cease." This passage concerns physical planting and harvest. But throughout the Bible you'll find that the law of the harvest applies to more than just the physical production of crops.

It applies to virtually every part of our lives, including man's moral behavior. "Do not be deceived: God cannot be mocked. A man reaps what he sows" (Galatians 6:7).

Another illustration of this law appears in Matthew 17. When Jesus' disciples were unable to cast out an evil spirit from a boy, He told them, "I tell you the truth, if you have faith as small as a mustard seed, you can say to this mountain, 'Move from here to there' and it will move. Nothing will be impossible for you" (vv. 20,21). Jesus' point is clear: If you sow even a tiny amount of faith, you will reap enormous spiritual results.

The Holy Spirit guided Paul to use harvest imagery to encourage us to become generous givers when Paul wrote, "Remember this: Whoever sows sparingly will also reap sparingly, and whoever sows generously will also reap generously" (2 Corinthians 9:6).

God Promises Rewards

Giving to the Lord is, in fact, a God-backed, guaranteed investment, not an uncertain gamble. Jesus uses the promise of reward to teach His followers. He teaches people to give without a public display because the glory should go to God, not man: "Then your Father, who sees what is done in secret, will reward you" (Matthew 6:4). God promises to reward the person who gives.

Jesus also teaches, "If anyone gives even a cup of cold water to one of these little ones because he is my disciple... he will certainly not lose his reward" (Matthew 10:42). Again, the Lord reinforces a cause-and-effect relationship between giving and receiving.

The healthy desire for rewards, with a proper motivation, is legitimate for Christians today. The classic text on faith, Hebrews 11:6, tells us that God "rewards those who earnestly seek him." In Matthew 6:19-34, Jesus compares giving to storing up treasures in heaven (v. 20). He tells His followers not to worry about the physical needs of life because God will take care of His children! This passage fits today, doesn't it? God longs for us to trust Him enough to "seek first his kingdom and his righteousness" (v. 33).

As we do, Jesus promises "all these things will be given to you as well" (v. 33). "All these things" includes such necessities of life as food and clothing. Jesus gives us permission to expect God to reward His children when we trust Him to provide.

God's teaching on generosity also is expressed with another principle: Trust God to reward true obedience. In general, it's easy to accept this principle in the Word of God. We see a number of examples verifying this idea throughout Scripture. We trust God to bless children who obey their parents in the Lord (Ephesians 6:1-3). We trust God to make "all things work together for good..." (Romans 8:28 KJV). And we trust God to save us when we commit our lives to Jesus (Hebrews 5:9). If we didn't believe God was trustworthy in keeping His promises and didn't believe His Word to be true, there would be little point in following Jesus.

Unfortunately, many Christians act as if this principle applies in all areas of life except in their financial dealings. Many Christians are convinced that they can't afford to give to God. The reason? Fear. It's one thing to believe in God; it's another to trust God to provide the rent payment. When you're engulfed in financial hardships, it's hard to think about giving. Yet "what is impossible with men is possible with God" (Luke 18:27). When God asks us to trust Him with our finances, He also promises to reward us. He doesn't always spell out the exact ways He will repay our trust, but He does promise us a rich reward so we can be generous to His purposes on every occasion (2 Corinthians 9:11).

Also understand that this is not what some have called the "health and wealth gospel." Any prosperity theology that attempts to turn God into some kind of "heavenly vending machine" is merely a selfish abuse of Scripture. God has promised rewards that include financial blessings, but we must be committed to following His purpose.

Specific Rewards We're Promised

God promises His children many rewards when we give. Here are three specific rewards:

Reward 1—You will be made rich in every way.

In his letter to the Corinthian church, Paul gives an interesting definition of the word "rich": "Now he who supplies seed to the sower and bread for food will also supply and increase your store of seed and will enlarge the harvest of your righteousness. You will be made rich in every way so that you can be generous on every occasion, and through us your generosity will result in thanksgiving to God" (2 Corinthians 9:10,11).

God's Word defines rich as "able to be generous." God's Word also says we'll be made rich in every way. This proves we should never limit the extent of God's blessing to the spiritual or emotional arena. God promises that if we give to Him, He will give us the financial capacity to be generous.

The Bible describes riches as both spiritual and material. Of all the riches we can possess, none of them is more important than spiritual riches. Scripture speaks about the riches of God's grace, God's glory, His understanding, His wisdom, and His insight. When we are generous givers, we have access to all of these riches.

Paul explains to the Corinthians that financial decisions have physical advantages as well. He isn't merely referring to the emotional or spiritual blessings we can receive from giving. He is saying that financial generosity leads to greater financial resources—even physical wealth! This is the clear, unbiased teaching of Scripture.

However, if you have the desire to be wealthy so that you can spend these resources on yourself, don't expect to claim this reward (1 Timothy 6:9,10). The so-called "health and wealth gospel" teaches that Christians should give to get. But God says we should give to get to give again. This represents a balanced "theology of generosity" (Titus 3:14).

I believe we have steered so far away from the ditch of the health and wealth gospel that we find ourselves in the opposite ditch on the other side of the road that says God does not work in our finances. We're hesitant to take God at His Word and believe or teach what Scripture teaches. The text says we'll be made rich in every way, which means we'll be able to share.

I spoke with a friend who is a successful businessman and an elder in his congregation. Over the years, he has counseled more than fifty couples who were in severe financial difficulty. When they came to him for advice about solving their money problems, he agreed to help if they would decide to give ten cents of every dollar they made to the Lord. My friend said every couple who followed through not only got their financial house in order, but they also had the opportunity to do good for God. That's a tremendous track record!

If deep in your heart you have the desire to be a good manager of God's resources and want to be generous in meeting needs so that people give thanks to God, then you must expect God to provide. Paul set the stage for the proper desires of our heart when he wrote, "For you know the grace of our Lord Jesus Christ, that though he was rich, yet for your sakes he became poor, so that you through his poverty might become rich" (2 Corinthians 8:9). It's difficult to twist the Scriptures into a selfish interpretation when you keep the focus on Jesus.

God doesn't oppose blessing His servants with material well-being, as long as they keep their desires and fortunes devoted to Him. First Chronicles 29:12 tells us that wealth comes from God. Passages like Joshua 1:8, Proverbs 3:9,10, and Malachi 3:10 will help us overcome our fears about God's provision.

The Old Testament clearly tells us that God made people wealthy like Abraham, Jacob, David, Solomon, Jehoshaphat, and Job. In the New Testament, we read of such wealthy believers as Joseph of Arimathea, Lydia, and others. If there were no wealthy Christians, there would be no need for this kind of teaching. If God hated material wealth, why would He grant physical riches as a reward to many of His people? God wants to reward His faithful, generous followers with both spiritual and material riches. I believe this is true because it is taught in God's Word.

Reward 2—You will receive more than you give.

When was the last time you read Luke 6:38? "Give, and it will be given to you. A good measure, pressed down, shaken together and running over, will be poured into your lap. For with the measure you use, it will be measured to you."

I have a confession to make. For far too long, I have simply not believed this passage. I have tried hard to find some way to get around the truth that is taught so clearly. I think my motivation was based partially on my opposition to what some call "prosperity gospel." Deep inside, however, I think my struggles with this passage really signaled my lack of faith in God to reward my obedient giving.

Jesus says to tap into God's economy. The Lord is a generous provider. You won't run out of money! Don't be afraid to give. When you give, you also receive "a good measure, pressed down, shaken together and running over, will be poured into your lap." I've never seen an exception to this rule. You always receive more than you give. If you give love, you receive more love. If you give friendship, you receive more friends in return. I've even noticed that if you give a smile to someone, you will receive more smiles. So it follows from Scripture and practical experience that if you give money, you receive more money.

For years I struggled with this text. I thought it was materialistic to think God would bless me financially when I gave money to do His work. In reality, the materialistic view is thinking that my own ingenuity is the only source of my ability to make money. A spiritual person obeys and trusts God to release His blessings and provide all the resources of life. The unspiritual person believes human effort is the source of material wealth.

Reward 3—You will receive a greater blessing.

Acts 20:35 shares a familiar quotation of our Lord: "It is more blessed to give than to receive." We all agree that it's a blessing to receive, but Jesus says it's an even greater blessing to give! However enjoyable you think receiving is, Jesus says giving is better—it is more blessed.

I've pondered Jesus' statement for years. How could giving bring a greater blessing? This made no sense to me, especially as a young child. Like most kids, I always hoped for a big haul under the tree on Christmas morning. I had my wish list and was never bashful about sharing it with my parents. My mother's standard reply to my childish, greedy nature was to quote Acts 20:35. It's no wonder I never cared much for that verse when I was a kid!

Now that I'm a parent, I've gained a fuller understanding about Jesus' teaching. First, I receive a greater blessing by helping someone and seeing their excitement or appreciation. Second, I receive a greater blessing by realizing that God has given me something to share. What if I were the one in need? Having something to share creates feelings of gratitude for God's provision. Third, I receive a greater blessing because I have something else to anticipate. Giving allows me to participate in God's economy, where my financial investments in His Kingdom generate remarkable returns.

A preacher friend of mine has a quick, three-point outline on giving that he drew from Galatians 6:7, "A man reaps what he sows." My friend's application: (1) you reap what you sow; (2) you reap more than you sow; and (3) you reap after you sow. When I use this Scripture to see how God works, I see giving in a different light. Giving is not an expense; it's an opportunity!

Of course, we were all touched by the stories of faith, generosity, and sacrifice from the relief efforts after hurricane Katrina devastated much of the Gulf Coast in August, 2005. Thousands of Christians responded with millions of dollars and countless hours of service to the hurt and needy. One very special story involved The Harvest, an Assemblies of God church in Slidell, Louisiana whose building was engulfed by flood waters, leaving this church of 1,100 with no place to meet. Doug McAllister, the pastor, gathered his staff together to let them know there was no money to pay salaries and he had to lay them off. His staff told him that God had called them to serve at that place and they would continue to serve the people in need, even without pay. When John Lindell, the pastor at James River Assembly in Ozark, Missouri, heard this, he and his leadership team immediately sent word that James River would pay the salaries of the staff for the next month while the pastor and the church worked out their next steps. What a great testimony of faith and service!

Receive Blessings "in Kind"

Both common sense and these passages imply that the type of seed you sow determines the kind of crop you will receive. If you sow corn, you will reap corn (Genesis 8:22). If you sow moral actions in your daily behavior, you will reap a moral life (Galatians 6:7). If you sow faith, you will reap faith (Matthew 17:20). If you sow financially, you will reap financially (2 Corinthians 9:6).

This teaching is well represented throughout the Bible. If you sow faith in Jesus Christ's atonement on the cross in obedience to the gospel, you reap eternal life. If you sow Bible study, you reap spiritual insight. In Scripture, there is an exact match between the kind of thing you sow and the kind of thing you reap. This same cause-and-effect principle applies to judging, condemning, and forgiving (Luke 6:37). Jesus promises "a good measure, pressed down, shaken together and running over..." (v. 38). Jesus wants us to know not only that we receive more than we give, but also that we receive the same kind of thing that we give. Jesus tells us that the amount and kind of gift we give determines the amount and kind of gift we receive. I have found no exception in Scripture to this insight.

Trust God to Provide

God's Word calls us to have faith in His promises. If we see Him as the Source of our blessings, we won't be afraid of running out of the physical resources we need. When you are facing too much month at the end of your money, remember God's promise to provide for your needs—and more.

One of the most fantastic accounts of God's provision comes from 2 Kings 4:1-7. A poor widow came to Elisha, the prophet, and cried out to him in despair. Creditors were threatening to take away her two sons as slaves to pay her debts. When Elisha asked what resources she possessed, the woman replied that she had only a small amount of oil. Elisha told her to go to all her neighbors and borrow as many of their empty jars as possible. Then she was to go inside and start pouring oil from her jar into the empty jars. Her sons brought jars to her, and she kept pouring until all the jars were full. When she poured her oil into the last jar, the oil stopped flowing. Elisha then told her to sell the oil to pay her debts and live on what was left.

Not only did God provide for her, but the amount of God's provision was in direct proportion to her trust—he gave her as much oil as she was prepared to receive. God will provide material blessings to meet our physical needs and gain our spiritual attention as well.

God's response to money problems is the same as His answer to health concerns, family problems, or any difficult circumstances. God wants us to trust Him, not our job or our bank balance. Jesus said, "For where your treasure is, there your heart will be also" (Matthew 6:21).

Since God wants our hearts, He works through our finances. When we learn to trust Him with our money, we will learn to trust Him with anything—even our very lives!

Think It Through

Word One: I Will Make You Rich in Every Way

1. Listed below are several of the resources commonly used to provide for the daily necessities of life. Which one do you depend on the most? Why?

Job	Savings	Education
Whom you know	Intellect	Good luck
Investments	Parents	Land
Appearance	Personality	Other:

2. What would you do if your primary resource was suddenly taken away?

3. Read the following passages and identify the general theme of each one.

   Passage   *Theme*

   Joshua 1:8

   Malachi 3:9-11

   Proverbs 3:9,10

   Luke 6:38

   Compare your answer for question 1 to these themes. Do your responses match?

4. If you were to see God as the true Source of your blessings, what first financial decision would you make?

Meditate on God's Word

Take God at His Word, and let the truths of these texts convince you that He will provide for you materially.

Joshua 1:8
Do not let this Book of the Law depart from your mouth; meditate on it day and night, so that you may be careful to do everything written in it. Then you will be prosperous and successful.

Luke 12:29
And do not set your heart on what you will eat or drink; do not worry about it.

Luke 12:31
But seek his kingdom, and these things will be given to you as well.

Philippians 4:6
Do not be anxious about anything, but in everything, by prayer and petition, with thanksgiving, present your requests to God.

Philippians 4:17-19
Not that I am looking for a gift, but I am looking for what may be credited to your account. I have received full payment and even more; I am amply supplied, now that I have received from Epaphroditus the gifts you sent. They are a fragrant offering, an acceptable sacrifice, pleasing to God. And my God will meet all your needs according to his glorious riches in Christ Jesus.

1 Timothy 6:17,18
Command those who are rich in this present world not be arrogant nor to put their hope in wealth, which is so uncertain, but to put their hope in God, who richly provides us with everything for our enjoyment. Command them to do good, to be rich in good deeds, and to be generous and willing to share.

Are you excited about this journey of faith you've read about? Ponder the possibilities and confirm your decision to trust God's Word as you pray.

Let's Pray...

Join with me in this prayer of commitment to the Lord:

Lord, I pause to proclaim to You that I know You are the Sovereign Ruler of this universe. I also know You are aware of all my needs. You are the Source of all my blessings too. But I need Your help so that I can trust You and tap into the rewards You promise through Your law of the harvest. I want to be blessed so I can bless others in Your name. I will take You at Your Word and make a commitment to obey the Scriptures. I also will wait with anticipation to see what You will do next because of Jesus. In His name I pray, amen.

Malachi 3:10

"*Bring the whole tithe into the storehouse, that there may be food in my house. Test me in this,*" *says the LORD Almighty,* "*and see if I will not throw open the floodgates of heaven and pour out so much blessing that you will not have room enough for it.*"

In the next few pages you'll discover:

❖ God invites us to take Him at His Word and test Him by tithing.

❖ Tithing is a doorway to God's blessings today.

❖ If you don't tithe, you may fall "under a curse."

WORD TWO
I Want You to Tithe So I Can Reward You

Throughout the years, God has released great blessings when His children wholeheartedly followed Him. If you "honor the LORD with your wealth, with the firstfruits of all your crops, then your barns will be filled to overflowing, and your vats will brim over with new wine" (Proverbs 3:9,10). What a great promise from Scripture! Do you realize that this inspired promise still applies to us today? After all, this promise comes just three verses after this great encouragement: "Trust in the Lord with all your heart and lean not on your own understanding; in all your ways acknowledge him, and he will make your paths straight." Since we can have confidence in our Father to give us wisdom and guidance in our daily lives, then why not trust Him completely to provide for us financially when we put Him first in our giving?

This chapter focuses on the incredible blessings that God has promised once we decide to give at least a tenth of our income back to God. Giving a tenth, also called "tithing," should actually be a starting point in our giving. The Bible clearly teaches that the Lord is looking to bless us as a result of our important step of faith.

The Book of Malachi reveals how important the tithe is to God. When His people refused to honor Him with their wealth, God actually accused them of stealing from Him:

"Will a man rob God? Yet you rob me.

"But you ask, 'How do we rob you?'

"In tithes and offerings. You are under a curse—the whole nation of you—because you are robbing me. Bring the whole tithe into the storehouse, that there may be food in my house. Test me in this," says the LORD Almighty, "and see if I will not throw open the floodgates of heaven and pour out so much blessing that you will not have room enough for it" (3:8-10).

God's Word says that when His people obeyed Him by tithing, He would shower them with material blessing. But when they refused to follow His wishes regarding their giving, the Bible says they fell "under a curse"!

Sometimes, Christians get swept up in a debate over whether or not we're required to tithe, when that's not the real question. The real question is, does the promise of Malachi 3:9,10 still apply today? I believe it does.

So, my question is, do you believe God will never destroy the earth by water again? How do you know? Your confidence is certainly based on the promise found in Genesis 9:12-16. In that passage God said,

This is the sign of the covenant I am making between me and you and every living creature with you, a covenant for all generations to come: I have set my rainbow in the clouds, and it will be the sign of the covenant between me and the earth. Whenever I bring clouds over the earth and the rainbow appears in the clouds, I will remember my covenant between me and you and all living creatures of every kind. Never again will the waters become a flood to destroy all life. Whenever the rainbow appears in the clouds, I will see it and remember the everlasting covenant between God and all living creatures of every kind on the earth.

This promise did not have to be restated in the New Testament in order to be valid today, just as the promise of Proverbs 3:5,6 about guidance did not have to be restated. God's promise in regard to tithing is no different. Our decision to give at least 10 percent of our income back to God reflects our reliance on Him as the Source of all our blessings. This kind of faith pleases the Lord and brings abundant blessing.

One of my all-time favorite stories on tithing comes from a church that was in the middle of using the *Take God at His Word* series. Brandon and Jenny were like most young families on a tight budget. But, this young family was also committed to tithing off the top, so they did that first, and then paid the rest of their bills. One particular week, Brandon griped to Ryan, another friend from church, that he only had three dollars left in his checking account and didn't even have enough money for the haircut he had scheduled the next day.

Ryan told him, "Hey, we've been talking about this at church. If you really need that haircut, God will see that you get it." Brandon laughed and said, "I guess so, but somebody's going to have to give me the money, or I'm going to have to go home and find it in the mailbox, because I don't have it."

When Brandon got home that afternoon, he opened up his mailbox and found a rebate check inside that he'd forgotten all about. It was for nine dollars, the exact price of his haircut. Brandon said, "I don't have any flashy stories about big money, but I did get a nine-dollar haircut!"

Later Brandon was putting on a pair of pants he hadn't worn in a while. He reached in his pocket and found twelve more dollars! "Gas money!" he said to himself.

You can choose to call that a coincidence if you want to, but I'm convinced that God delights in giving to His children. Once in a while, He also makes it come out dead even—like a nine dollar haircut—just so we don't miss the point.

Let's not require the New Testament to explicitly command us to tithe before we use this simple measure as a generosity standard. We could miss God's richest blessings.

Power Principles of Tithing

Both biblical principles and practical experiences demonstrate the power of tithing in a Christian's life. What will happen when we take Him at His Word and tithe as a starting point for giving? I've noticed four major results, all biblical principles that provide a practical foundation for tithing today.

Power Principle 1—
Tithing motivates greater faithfulness.

Did you know that Jesus actually taught His followers to live by a higher standard than the one given in the Old Testament? Obviously, we, too, want to please Him and be faithful to His call. Jesus contrasted the requirements of the Law with the plan for His followers.

The following chart cites several examples and raises the question: which is the higher standard, the Law of Moses or the Way of Christ?

Old Testament	*New Testament*
Do not murder.	Anyone who
(Exodus 20:13)	hates his brother
	is a murderer.
	(1 John 3:15)

Do not commit adultery. (Exodus 20:14)	Anyone who lusts commits adultery in his heart. (Matthew 5:28)
Do not swear falsely by God's name. (Leviticus 19:12)	Do not swear at all. (Matthew 5:34)
The entire tithe will be holy to the LORD. (Leviticus 27:32)	Give as you are prospered. (1 Corinthians 16:2)

An exhaustive study of the Scriptures reveals this often overlooked truth: Jesus' way always calls for greater faithfulness and commitment than was required in the Old Testament. Can giving possibly be an exception? It follows clearly that no one who wants to be faithful to God would ever think of doing less than the Old Testament believers. Remember, Christ came to fulfill the Law, not to destroy it (Matthew 5:17). And Hebrews 10:1 says, "The law is only a shadow of the good things that are coming— not the realities themselves."

Jesus came to bring us "the good things." If we want these things in our life, then we must sow the seed necessary to reap them. His Word teaches that faithfulness in tithing is one of the pathways to receiving the spiritual and physical blessings He desires for us.

It amazed me when I learned that tithing was not unique to God's chosen people. Other ancient civilizations also practiced giving a tenth of their income to various pagan deities. Archaeological research indicates that the people of Egypt, Babylon, and Assyria also tithed. Imagine that! Both Jewish followers of God and pagans devoted to false deities saw that spiritual faithfulness included tithing.

Dr. John Willis, a distinguished professor of Old Testament studies, has written a profound paper on tithing. In it he says:

> By giving their tithes, the Israelites were proclaiming that they were giving back to the Lord a portion of that which He had prospered them (Deuteronomy 26:10-15). Just as God had given His people the food and resources they needed for their existence, by tithing the people were imitating Him by giving their God-given food and resources to the slaves, the poor, the sojourners, the orphans, and the widows. Thus, tithing was the means God gave the Israelites to express their love to God for all He had given them (Deuteronomy 6:4-9) and to express their love to their neighbor as God had expressed His love to them (Leviticus 19:18).[2]

Surely, as recipients of "the good things," it's also clear that the Lord has commissioned us to do the same today!

Power Principle 2—
Tithing releases God's financial blessings!

Talk about needed power! This principle is where the "rubber of faith meets the road of reality." It's also where the Lord has an opportunity to shine on us and empower us to better reflect His glory, as Thomas Trask put it so eloquently:

> God does not expect His people to live in want. Often He even grants us the desires of our heart and blesses us beyond measure. Yet, if our priorities are as they should be, we will not be caught up in gaining more and more for our own gratification, but be compelled to invest our resources, whether great or small, back into the Kingdom of God. We do this

by supporting the ministries of the church, giving to world and home missions, funding special outreaches to the needy among us, and more. When we do this, God is pleased to increase His blessings toward us, for the biblical principle is this:

"Give, and it will be given to you. A good measure, pressed down, shaken together and running over, will be poured into your lap. For with the measure you use, it will be measured to you" (Luke 6:38). We cannot outgive God.

With that encouragement in mind, let's return to Malachi 3:10. God's Word says, "'Bring the whole tithe into the storehouse, that there may be food in my house. Test me in this,' says the LORD Almighty, 'and see if I will not throw open the floodgates of heaven and pour out so much blessing that you will not have room enough for it.'" This is one of the most remarkable passages in the whole Bible. The God of the universe actually told His people to test Him. The Hebrew word for "test" means to examine. God said they could check Him out and see if He was telling the truth. This is the only time in Scripture when God allowed His creation to see if He really would keep His Word. The Lord told them that if they would once again put Him first and prove their loyal devotion to Him by bringing in their whole tithe, He would drench them with material blessings. They could go to the bank on this promise.

I am convinced that God will do the same today. I know many people who have taken God at His Word and tithed when they didn't know how they possibly could. One Christian I know who had never tithed before began tithing, and, for no apparent reason, His business quadrupled. He said he believed God was the Source of his blessing, because he hadn't changed any of his business practices. In fact, this man was even working fewer hours.

What if you are financially strapped? One of the young, single-parent moms in a church where I preached determined to tithe, even though she couldn't cover her current monthly expenses. She signed a pledge card, not knowing where the money would come from. Two days later, her boss called her into his office unexpectedly. He praised her work and gave her a 13 percent raise on the spot! While excited about the raise, she was overjoyed at the realization that God had come through!

Now, after years of listening to the faith stories of others, I have yet to hear of a single story where God did not abundantly bless obedient, grateful love like this. Just remember, we don't give to be blessed, we give because we are blessed. Tithing declares our realization that God has already blessed us, as well as our conviction that He will continue to take care of us.

Power Principle 3—
Tithing expands evangelical Kingdom work.

According to current research in churches across America, the average percentage of giving per Christian is less than 2 percent. It doesn't take a mathematical genius to see that church-wide tithing would allow ministry efforts to virtually explode. Imagine how much greater God would be glorified if the Kingdom of Christ quadrupled its resources! You allow God to have a greater influence in the world around you when you honor Him with your financial tithe.

I preached as a guest speaker in a congregation that only two years ago struggled to pay the bills. They began to emphasize taking God at His Word and strongly encouraged the members to begin tithing. In a matter of weeks, their giving boomed, and the morale in the church skyrocketed. New plans and ministries began to sprout, involvement increased dramatically, and the ministry impact on the community expanded with a fresh vision. They continued to stretch, and now their weekly budget is almost twice what it was before they realized the link between trusting God and giving. This is now an excited church! Tithing provides abundant resources to do ministry.

Power Principle 4—
Tithing changes spending habits.

If your giving standard has been low, starting to tithe may seem to stretch you financially at first. But in the process of tithing, you learn to prioritize your spending patterns and develop a sound financial budget. This will give you more money to give. You'll also find that the discipline brought on by tithing will help you fight the materialistic urges prompted by the marketing gurus of our consumer-driven society.

People who are committed to tithing evaluate their spending habits more closely. They follow spiritually and financially healthy practices that protect their ability to trust God to provide for them. These practices include setting aside their weekly offering first, making purchasing decisions in light of how those decisions will impact their offering to the Lord, and thinking about what they really need versus what they think they need. It's a lot like establishing a good nutrition plan—when you eat right, you stay healthier and happier. In the same way, when you establish a solid commitment to tithe, you will trim the fat out of your spending, leaving more for the Kingdom and more for you to spend wisely.

Living Under a Curse

The other side of this opportunity is a question: What happens if you don't take God at His Word in tithing? To see what can happen, look at the Book of Malachi. Chapters one through three of Malachi illustrated the wicked state of affairs in Israel. The hearts of the people and their priests were corrupt. They were plagued with sin, divorce, and social injustice. Malachi 3:9 reveals that they were under a curse simply because they failed to honor God with their tithe.

These are chilling words. The Bible uses the word "curse" to describe the fruit of their unfaithfulness toward God and His purposes for them. The grammatical structure of this phrase in Hebrew is even more shocking. This passage says literally that God's people were "cursed with a curse."

When you look at the definition of "curse" and see how it is used in other passages in Scripture, it clearly refers to the experience of God either bringing punishment or withholding blessing. For example, Malachi 2:2 says, " 'If you do not listen, and if you do not set your heart to honor my name,' says the LORD Almighty, 'I will send a curse upon you, and I will curse your blessings. Yes, I have already cursed them, because you have not set your heart to honor me. ' "

Think of the many ways that you could be "under a curse" and have to endure a situation that you know is not God's best. Perhaps your relationship with a loved one is in shambles, or your business opportunities seem extremely limited, or it could be that Jesus doesn't seem real to you. On the other hand, wouldn't you like to experience the favor of God in your life? God clearly pronounces both spiritual and physical blessings on those who follow His will. God's blessings affect life's happiness, finances, government, and longevity of life. The following passages give you a brief sample of how God withholds curses and releases blessings.

Psalm 128:1-4

Blessed are all who fear the LORD, who walk in his ways. You will eat the fruit of your labor; blessings and prosperity will be yours. Your wife will be like a fruitful vine within your house; your sons will be like olive shoots around your table. Thus is the man blessed who fears the LORD.

Proverbs 10:22

The blessing of the LORD brings wealth, and he adds no trouble to it.

Proverbs 11:11

Through the blessing of the upright a city is exalted, but by the mouth of the wicked it is destroyed.

Ephesians 6:1-3

Children, obey your parents in the Lord, for this is right. "Honor your father and mother"—which is the first commandment with a promise — "that it may go well with you and that you may enjoy long life on the earth."

James 1:12

Blessed is the man who perseveres under trial, because when he has stood the test, he will receive the crown of life that God has promised to those who love him.

The Lord also wants to bring many kinds of practical, physical blessings to us:

- He wants to give His people productive and prosperous businesses (Psalm 128:2).
- He wants us to experience joy in marriage (Psalm 128:3).
- He wants us to delight in parenting our children (Psalm 128:3).

- He desires that we benefit from a long life (Ephesians 6:1-3).

- He wants to give us strength and hope in times of adversity (James 1:12).

These represent only a few of the ways that God wants to bring tangible, personal favor into the lives of His people. They illustrate the "fruit of righteousness" that can be ours as a result of an obedient, loving trust in God. Ever since my children were young, I have used a little quote to help them learn to obey me. I told them over and over, "If you obey, good things happen; if you disobey, bad things happen. Which one do you want?" They always answered, "Good things." Then I said, "So what should you do?" I am sure you can predict their answer. (By the way, they can quote my little phrase at the drop of a hat!) While this little phrase never created perfect obedience, it did help them to see that all behavior has consequences.

God deals with us in the same way. He wants us to learn to trust Him without question or hesitation. When we trust and follow Him, He never fails to keep His promises of blessing. But because our sinful nature gives us tendencies to be stubborn and selfish, we often need positive reinforcement to help us learn to obey and punishment when we disobey. It is not an enjoyable concept to teach, but the Bible tells us that when we do not take God at His Word in any area of life, we put ourselves at risk of falling under a "curse" just as the Israelites did in Malachi 3.

To illustrate, I will point out a few more passages where God warns His people that failure to cooperate with His plan exposes them to the results of some type of curse—meaning possible discipline, punishment, or judgment.

In Genesis 3:17, God cursed the ground after casting Adam and Eve from the Garden of Eden. The effect of this curse is that Adam would always find it difficult to raise crops. Had he and Eve kept the Lord's commands, they could have stayed in the beautiful paradise where fruit was plentiful and easy to reach.

In Genesis 4:11,12, God cursed Cain for murdering his brother Abel. The effect of this curse was that Cain became a wandering outcast who would always struggle to survive.

In Genesis 12:3, God promised to bless anyone who blessed Abraham and curse anyone who cursed him. While we have no specific details of how God applied the blessings or the curses, several stories in Abraham's later life indicate that God brought good things to Abraham's allies and bad things to those who opposed Him.

In Deuteronomy 27 and 28, God warned the Israelites that failure to obey all of His commandments would result in their being cursed. In these passages, this meant that they would have problems bearing children, growing crops, raising livestock, and so on. These very real, daily life situations helped Israel to see that God meant business.

As you read through these examples, you probably concluded (as I have) that being "cursed with a curse" means basically, "You are in big trouble with God."

If there is an area in your life in which you are continually defeated, this may be God's merciful way of getting your attention. It may be time to determine if the root of that problem is your inattention to God's promises, which are linked to your eligibility to receive a blessing. That is exactly what Malachi was trying to communicate.

This principle is also why I believe curses still occur today.

A brilliant, young electrical engineer, whose life was in trouble, wrote a letter sharing his experience. Here's an excerpt that I have received permission to share:

> As you know, I came to this church a very hurting person. I carried burdens that left me completely helpless. I was existing, but not really living. Three years ago, I grew gravely ill and lost most of my physical strength and much of my immune system. At my lowest point, I literally crawled across my front lawn to get to my car because I was too weak to walk. I felt that I was dying, and I was morbidly afraid of death and literally terrified of going to hell. I was out of touch with God. I felt if I could just find another doctor, surely everything would get better.
>
> Then, in desperation, without asking for anything specific, I cried out to God to help me. "Please God," I prayed, "do something to let me know You're here." I was ready to do anything. Now I know that God was humbling me so that I would come to trust Him more completely. On my first visit [to church], I was astonished! Even though this congregation is very large, I felt comfortable here immediately. I felt a keen sense of the presence of God which I had never felt anywhere else. [The minister] is an inspired preacher. His sermons are always helpful, but the moment of truth came when he preached a sermon on stewardship and said, "Anyone who does not give back to God 10 percent of his income is a thief." I had never even seriously thought of giving 10 percent and couldn't imagine how in the world that could possibly fit into my tight budget.

But the word "thief" hit me hard, as the truth always does. I now realize that I was so miserable precisely because God was last on my list of priorities rather than first. So I asked God's forgiveness, and I pledged to give back 10 percent of my income for the rest of my life. This is the most important decision I have ever made.

From that moment, things began to change dramatically for the better. The people who are closest to me have marveled at the changes in my life. Too many positive things have happened to be coincidence. Most obvious is my greatly improved health, which has been immediate. Most practical is that after looking for a job for three years, I found one—the best job I've ever had in my life! Most gratifying is the deep feeling of inner peace, which I feel for the first time in my life. I feel different on the inside than when I first came to see you, and everybody who knows me says I'm different on the outside too.

What a testimony to God's Word! If you're experiencing great financial difficulty, have you considered the possibility that you might be living under an easily reversible curse? The Word of God is full of verses that show how disobeying God leads to a number of curses.

Failing to tithe places you in the same curse-risk category as committing more familiar and obvious sins, such as refusing to repent, disrespecting parents, stealing, or lying.

The principle of tithing is simple. Thankfully, the Lord is "a forgiving God, gracious and compassionate, slow to anger and abounding in love..." (Nehemiah 9:17). No matter your past experience with tithing, it is never too late to take God at

His Word. If you tithe, you will receive God's blessings. If you don't tithe, you rob God and you cheat yourself.

God releases His power when we put our faith in Him. Take Him at His Word, and He will respond with blessing. The Word says:

> If any of you lacks wisdom, he should ask God, who gives generously to all without finding fault, and it will be given to him. But when he asks, he must believe and not doubt, because he who doubts is like a wave of the sea, blown and tossed by the wind. That man should not think he will receive anything from the Lord; he is a double-minded man, unstable in all he does (James 1:5-8).

Avoid double-minded thinking. Let faith take charge of your heart as you take hold of God's promises. It's not a matter of whether or not you can afford to tithe, it's whether or not you can afford *not* to. When you put the Lord first, He promises to open up heaven and pour out His blessings.

Think It Through

Word Two: I Want You to Tithe So I Can Reward You

1. Read each passage about God's Kingdom and contrast it with the world's mind-set:

   1 Chronicles 29:12

   Psalm 50:9,10

   Proverbs 3:9,10
   Proverbs 10:22

   1 Timothy 6:6-10

2. If someone were to ask you for advice about tithing, what would you tell them?

3. How did the story about the young engineer (pp. 31-33) make you feel? Why?

4. Brainstorm a few blessings that might come if you "put God to the test" (Malachi 3:10)?

Meditate on God's Word

God already owns everything, so why does He want us to give? These passages reveal His desire for us to trust Him for all our needs and desire to be generous like Him. As you read these texts, ask yourself if your thinking reflects the mind-set of this world or of God's Kingdom.

Genesis 28:20-22

Then Jacob made a vow, saying, "If God will be with me and will watch over me on this journey I am taking and will give me food to eat and clothes to wear so that I return safely to my father's house, then the LORD will be my God and this stone that I have set up as a pillar will be God's house, and of all that you give me I will give you a tenth."

Deuteronomy 8:17,18

You may say to yourself, "My power and the strength of my hands have produced this wealth for me." But remember the LORD your God, for it is he who gives you the ability to produce wealth, and so confirms his covenant, which he swore to your forefathers, as it is today.

Proverbs 3:9,10

Honor the LORD with your wealth, with the firstfruits of all your crops; then your barns will be filled to overflowing, and your vats will brim over with new wine.

Proverbs 28:27

He who gives to the poor will lack nothing, but he who closes his eyes to them receives many curses.

2 Chronicles 31:5

As soon as the order went out, the Israelites generously gave the firstfruits of their grain, new wine, oil and honey and all that the fields produced. They brought a great amount, a tithe of everything.

Malachi 3:6-12

"I the LORD do not change. So you, O descendants of Jacob, are not destroyed. Ever since the time of your forefathers you have turned away from my decrees and have not kept them. Return to me, and I will return to you," says the LORD Almighty.

"But you ask, 'How are we to return?'

"Will a man rob God? Yet you rob me.

"But you ask, 'How do we rob you?'

"In tithes and offerings. You are under a curse—the whole nation of you—because you are robbing me. Bring the whole tithe into the storehouse, that there may be food in my house. Test me in this," says the LORD Almighty, "and see if I will not throw open the floodgates of heaven and pour out so much blessing that you will not have room enough for it. I will prevent pests from devouring your crops, and the vines in your fields will not cast their fruit," says the LORD Almighty. "Then all the nations will call you blessed, for yours will be a delightful land," says the LORD Almighty.

Malachi 3:17-18

"They will be mine," says the LORD Almighty, "in the day when I make up my treasured possessions. I will spare them, just as in compassion a man spares his son who serves him. And you will again see the distinction between the righteous and the wicked, between those who serve God and those who do not." [Author's Note: This passage is clearly referring to a later "Messianic" time. It points the way to Jesus and describes God's plans for the Church. There should always be a clear distinction between the Lord's people and those who are not. This distinction includes attitudes toward money and giving, but is not limited to this topic.]

Luke 6:38

Give, and it will be given to you. A good measure, pressed down, shaken together and running over, will be poured into your lap. For with the measure you use, it will be measured to you.

Galatians 6:9

Let us not become weary in doing good, for at the proper time we will reap a harvest if we do not give up.

Philippians 4:12-19

I know what it is to be in need, and I know what it is to have plenty. I have learned the secret of being content in any and every situation, whether well fed or hungry, whether living in plenty or in want. I can do everything through him who gives me strength.

Yet it was good of you to share in my troubles. Moreover, as you Philippians know, in the early days of your acquaintance with the gospel, when I set out from Macedonia, not one church shared with me in the matter of giving and receiving, except you only; for even when I was in Thessalonica, you sent me aid again and again when I was in need. Not that I am looking for a gift, but I am looking for what may be credited to your account. I have received full payment and even more; I am amply supplied, now that I have received from Epaphroditus the gifts you sent. They are a fragrant offering, an acceptable sacrifice, pleasing to God. And my God will meet all your needs according to his glorious riches in Christ Jesus.

Hebrews 13:5,16

Keep your lives free from the love of money and be content with what you have, because God has said, "Never will I leave you; never will I forsake you."

And do not forget to do good and to share with others, for with such sacrifices God is pleased.

God's promises are exciting and amazing. Are you ready to "test Him" by tithing? Decide now to stand on His revealed promises and pray with assurance that He is listening closely to your words ... and your heart.

Let's Pray ...

Join with me in this prayer:

Holy Father, You have humbled me today. I want to honor You with my words of devotion and trust, but I must confess that the pull of the world's economic system is strong. Help me put my full weight down on Your promises to "throw open the floodgates of heaven and pour out so much blessing" that I truly do not have room for it. Sometimes this is hard for me to believe, but with the power of Your risen Son working in my heart, I will trust and obey! Thank You in advance for what You will do because You love me. In Jesus' name. Amen.

1 Timothy 6:17-19

Command those who are rich in this present world not to be arrogant nor to put their hope in wealth, which is so uncertain, but to put their hope in God, who richly provides us with everything for our enjoyment. Command them to do good, to be rich in good deeds, and to be generous and willing to share. In this way they will lay up treasure for themselves as a firm foundation for the coming age, so that they may take hold of life that is truly life.

In the next few pages you'll discover:

- ❖ God owns everything; you are one of His managers.
- ❖ Giving "tithes and offerings" ensures your continued reception of God's blessings.
- ❖ Being a generous manager of God's resources shows your quality of love for Him.

WORD THREE
I Trust You to Manage Material Resources

There are three types of givers. The first is like flint. You have to strike it to produce a spark. The second is like a sponge because you have to squeeze it to turn loose what's inside. The third is like a honeycomb. Its contents just ooze out all over!

Which one best describes you? If you want to experience God's blessing, you'll be like the honeycomb and let your resources flow out as a part of your nature. And you'll put God in control of your finances.

First, it is vital to understand a key money management principle: God owns everything (Psalm 50:10). Everything we possess is merely on loan from Him so that we can use His resources to bring Him glory and expand His Kingdom. He has given us our abilities to make a living (Deuteronomy 8:17,18).

Understanding that I have the honor of managing some of His material resources also has helped me see that I can take God at His Word.

Since we are managers, it follows that we should follow the instructions of our Owner. One of God's important principles is, "Whoever can be trusted with very little can also be trusted with much." This passage in Luke 16:10 shows us that the Lord entrusts more and more of His material resources to us as we prove we can be trusted to manage them effectively. This is one of the reasons why God has always wanted His people to be generous in giving money to do work that pleases Him. It's a form of spiritual resource management.

Throughout the Bible, God's people made offerings in order to support ministry projects and programs, like the famine relief to Jerusalem (Romans 15:25,26) and the care of widows (1 Timothy 5:16). God's people also gave to construct and maintain facilities for worship (Exodus 25:1-8; 2 Kings 12:5). Throughout both Testaments, the Lord's faithful contributed money to support the physical needs of leaders, teachers, and workers in God's service (Deuteronomy 18:1; Philippians 4:15; 1 Timothy 5:17,18).

The spirit of boundless generosity flows throughout the Old and New Testament scriptures. Two passages illustrate this well—Exodus 36:4-7 and 2 Corinthians 8:3-5. They both reveal the giving heart God seeks.

> So all the skilled craftsmen who were doing all the work on the sanctuary left their work and said to Moses, "The people are bringing more than enough for doing the work the LORD commanded to be done."
>
> Then Moses gave an order and they sent this word throughout the camp: "No man or woman is to make anything else as an offering for the sanctuary." And so the people were restrained from bringing more, because what they already had was more than enough to do all the work (Exodus 36:4-7).
>
> For I testify that they gave as much as they were able, and even beyond their ability. Entirely on their own, they urgently pleaded with us for the privilege of sharing in this service to the saints.
>
> And they did not do as we expected, but they gave themselves first to the Lord and then to us in keeping with God's will (2 Corinthians 8:3-5).

God wants His people to experience the privilege of giving—even those in poverty. All financial decisions are actually spiritual decisions. And when we put God first in our giving, we are involved in an act of worship to the Almighty.

It's Time to Decide

Do you long for the opportunity to worship God with wholehearted devotion? Do you give generously for a couple of weeks, and then start slacking off gradually? Remember, Satan is very clever. He stops at nothing to keep you from taking God at His Word, from trusting Him to reward your faithfulness. Make the following three specific decisions, no matter what your financial situation might be, and Satan will fail. God will ensure your success because He is the Source of your blessing!

Decision 1—Give to the Lord this Sunday.

Make this Sunday the day you take a bold step of faith, and follow God with your finances. First Corinthians provides specific, helpful insight. "Now about the collection for God's people: Do what I told the Galatian churches to do. On the first day of every week, each one of you should set aside a sum of money in keeping with his income, saving it up, so that when I come no collections will have to be made" (16:1,2).

If you are not already taking God at His Word in your giving, you must start this Sunday. Do not wait another week. The devil wants to deceive you into missing God's blessings as long as he can. Resist him by deciding right now to make a generous offering. Paul leaves no room for doubt. Everyone is to be involved because everyone has some kind of income. Even children can give a portion of their allowances to do

God's work. Children who learn to give when they're young will grow up trusting the Lord with their finances. Just think of how many debt and spending traps they will avoid!

Recently, a young man in his late teens heard a series of messages on this subject and realized he had not been giving as God had blessed him. The conviction he felt was so great that he went to his grandmother and said, "Grandma, I haven't been doing right by God in my giving." The following Sunday he placed a check for $1,000 in the collection plate! That's the kind of devotion that Zacchaeus demonstrated when he realized his failure to honor the Lord with his financial resources. When he realized that his life needed to be given over to God, he declared, "Look, Lord! Here and now I give half of my possessions to the poor, and if I have cheated anybody out of anything, I will pay back four times the amount" (Luke 19:8). That story has always fascinated me. Now I have a modern-day example to share too.

Decision 2—Give to the Lord every Sunday.

Since Paul is responding to their questions about when and how to give, these instructions also give wise counsel about the frequency of giving. Paul's inspired wisdom tells us to give "on the first day of every week" (1 Corinthians 16:2). Paul wanted their offerings "stored up" so no special collections would be necessary after he arrived. He knew the power of saving. A larger gift would be possible if the people set aside money regularly. Plus, the people were building a healthy, spiritual habit.

Decision 3—Plan to give "tithes and offerings."

When Paul tells the church at Corinth to "set aside a sum of money in keeping with his income" (v. 2), he gives no legislated amount for the Christian to give. There's no statement about percentages or specific monetary figures in any of the New Testament passages. But remember, the Old Testament was written "to teach us" (Romans 15:4) and thoroughly equip us for every good work (2 Timothy 3:17). In the Old Testament the primary use of the tithe was to support the priests and ongoing worship activities of the people of God. Their offerings were given in addition to their tithes and were used for special purposes.

This Old Testament principle of "tithes and offerings" is an effective biblical way to develop your own giving plan today. Some priorities should receive attention in your plan.

Give to the Lord first. This idea of firstfruits is found in Proverbs 3:9, 10. It teaches that giving the first part of the crop as it came in was a sign of trust in the Lord's provision. The Israelites had no way of knowing on their own if the rest of the crop would come in. They had to trust God. This text says they would receive a great harvest if they honored God with their wealth.

Several years ago, I was talking with a young man about giving. He shared the struggles he and his wife had about giving, despite his good job. Typically, they waited until late in the month to write their offering check. Like most young couples, they were usually strapped for funds by the end of the month, having little left for the Lord's work.

I know how easily couples can fall into this situation, so I casually mentioned how my wife and I give 10 percent. We literally write our checks to the church first, even before our house payment. Even though I am paid twice a month, we write four checks because we want to stay in the habit of making weekly offerings. I told him that this figure is built into our budget. I found out later that this young man went home that night and told his wife about our discussion. They decided to start writing out their offerings before they wrote any other checks. Giving the "firstfruits" of their income enabled both their offering and their faith to grow dramatically.

Tithe to your home congregation. In the Old Testament, God wanted the center of Jewish worship and spiritual leadership strong. God's people brought their tithes and offerings to the priests (Deuteronomy 12:5,6). This practice parallels the teaching of 1 Corinthians 16:2, where the church contributions were "set aside" and used for ministry. Today, as well, your home congregation needs to be financially strong. It's where you receive the greatest blessing. It's where your kids go to Sunday school, where your ministry has its greatest focus, and where you share in your closest friendships. It's where you remain most involved and receive the greatest spiritual nurturing. When you give to bless your home congregation, you, in turn, are blessed in many ways.

Recently, a preacher friend of mine was talking to me about using this book and teaching the series in his congregation. He also told me that a group of young leaders in his church came to him with a desire to start a new prayer emphasis. He asked me if *Take God at His Word* would fit in with this plan. I responded positively by saying that over the years I have noticed two areas of church life that bring renewal and excitement: strong prayer and strong giving. When committed to both, a church will feel a spirit of love, optimism, and expectancy. Visitors feel more welcome, evangelism explodes, and ministries expand as we shift our focus from ourselves back to God and onto the needs of people. God's blessings flow, and the devil is defeated on many fronts. After all, he cannot win many battles when he's up against the one-two punch of powerful prayer and generous giving.

Give extra offerings as the Lord prompts your heart. Don't ever feel limited to giving 10 percent. Our goal should be to "excel in this grace of giving" (2 Corinthians 8:7). Sometimes you have more to give and sometimes you have less. What should you do? Another Old Testament example says, "Tell the Israelites to bring me an offering. You are to receive the offering for me from each man whose heart prompts him to give" (Exodus 25:2).

This passage, from God's instructions on the building of the tabernacle, illustrates the Lord's desire to see us choose to give more when there's a special reason. In the Exodus story, the people gave so much that Moses had to tell them to stop. This extravagant response to God's work is important today too.

I have another good friend who has tithed for a number of years. About a year and a half ago, he and his wife felt convicted to go beyond tithing and give additional offerings. The Lord honored their faith in a marvelous way. First, God helped them to change their attitudes toward money and spending. They stopped focusing on their own pleasures and started looking for ways to serve God with the resources He entrusted to them.

Secondly, my friend saw a remarkable thing happen that year. Even though he was less busy, his income literally tripled. He is now convinced that God tries to find good people He can use by giving them money. This couple has learned that many Christians don't have enough simply because they don't give enough. Giving offerings above the tithe is a specific way to take Jesus at His Word. They are receiving a blessing that is "pressed down, shaken together and running over."

Church building projects are among the most frequent occasions when offerings are important. Effective, spiritually motivated churches shy away from making this time a mere fund-raising experience. Instead, they ask their members to pray about "what God wants to give through them." Since

God already owns everything, what could be a more accurate way of looking at giving?

This transforms the entire process into a "faith raising" experience. For example, personal friends and colleagues of mine like Del Rogers, Roger Lane, and Larry Russell are veteran leaders of hundreds, if not thousands, of successful church stewardship campaigns. In every case, these men (and other faithful "stewardship coaches" like them) encourage people to pray and seek God's will before making a decision during a capital stewardship campaign. The results and stories they've heard show how God touches hearts and changes lives. These stories include testimonies of people putting God first in these projects, "over and above" their tithes and regular offerings.

Here are a few ways people give "over and above" as they pray, "Lord, what do You want to do through my life to impact my church and its future?"

Consider these different ways to give:
1. "Extra" cash
2. Extra time (by making a 36-month commitment)
3. Assets including land, jewelry, and equipment
4. Life insurance
5. Stocks and bonds
6. Through wills and estates
7. Reduced living expenses
8. Second jobs
9. Postponement of major purchases
10. Redirecting completed car payments, mortgage payments or other installments

The list continues but the common theme remains: believers pray and take a step of faith. They know God will honor their desire to see the Kingdom expand and their faith grow. More than anything, they see the money they give as an investment in the will, ways, and work of a God who is faithful.

It's truly amazing what people have the courage to do after they pray. For me, it's fun to give extra offerings. Karen and I pray for wisdom and the resources to share in what God is doing through us. Then we choose special benevolence needs, new missions opportunities, building projects, or other special ministries to bless. Watching our money make a difference is a reward in itself. As we give, we always remember that we are "sowing seed" into people and ministries that will reap a harvest. Part of this harvest, Paul said in Philippians 4:17, is "credited to our account" in heaven too!

Remember your motives. The materialistic urges of modern society continually wear at the foundations of a God-given desire to make giving a top priority. That's why you must keep two reasons to give in the forefront of your consciousness.

First, remember tithes and offerings are a doorway to God's blessing. His desire is to pour out blessings from heaven (Malachi 3:10), to give back to you "a good measure, pressed down, shaken together and running over" (Luke 6:38), and to meet all of your needs (Philippians 4:19). God warned His people, "You will sow much seed in the field but you will harvest little, because locusts will devour it" (Deuteronomy 28:38). Refuse to let Satan steal your joy or your blessing. Keep the channel of God's blessing open. Remember that our motives must never be "give to get" but "give to get to give again." God's heart is to care for our need, not our greed. His plan is to build our faith and to empower us so that we can serve in His name.

Second, remember that tithes and offerings are a tremendous checkpoint to monitor the level of your obedience.

Tithing is not the end of our commitment to God in our giving—personal ministry is God's plan. Paul reminds Timothy, "Command those who are rich in this present world not to be arrogant nor to put their hope in wealth, which is so uncertain, but to put their hope in God, who richly provides us with everything for our enjoyment. Command them to do good, to be rich in good deeds, and to be generous and willing to share" (1 Timothy 6:17,18).

As you determine that you want to "give to get to give again," God will bring more and more people and needs into your life for you to touch financially. Resist the temptation to write these requests off as "black holes." Instead, pray over each opportunity and ask yourself, "Is God bringing this need into my life to help me grow in faith and service?" If He is, you will already have built into your spending patterns the habit that allows you to obey out of generosity and love.

Earlier this year, I had lunch with a pastor friend who was telling me about the results of his congregation's new-found commitment to giving and how it was affecting their plans for 2005. I was especially attentive to his reports of God's work because his church had used the *Take God at His Word* program in late fall 2004. It was time to find out what God was doing! With great excitement, he told me that their giving had increased so dramatically that, for the first time in their history, every ministry received the full amount of funds requested for the 2005 program of work, and they still had $150,000 to pay down their facility's mortgage. With this type of enthusiasm, giving, and commitment to the Lord's work and to serving people, only the Lord knows how much impact this church will have on its community.

Think It Through

Word Three:
I Trust You to Manage Material Resources

1. How often does your current approach to giving match the decisions suggested in this chapter?

2. As you read these three passages, focus on the attitudes you think God wants His children to develop. List as many as you can.

   Malachi 3:10

   Luke 6:38

   2 Corinthians 9:6-12

3. Word Three encourages you to make three decisions. Read each decision and circle the number from 1 (never) to 10 (always) that best describes your current giving practices.

   Decision 1—Give to the Lord this Sunday.

   1 2 3 4 5 6 7 8 9 10

   Decision 2—Give to the Lord every Sunday.

   1 2 3 4 5 6 7 8 9 10

   Decision 3—Plan to give "tithes and offerings."

   1 2 3 4 5 6 7 8 9 10

4. James 1:5 tells us that if we ask God for wisdom, He will give it generously. Make time now to ask God to grant you wisdom in your giving decisions, and listen for the new wisdom that God will provide.

Meditate On God's Word

Luke 16:10,11

Whoever can be trusted with very little can also be trusted with much, and whoever is dishonest with very little will also be dishonest with much. So if you have not been trustworthy in handling worldly wealth, who will trust you with true riches?

1 Corinthians 16:1,2

Now about the collection for God's people: Do what I told the Galatian churches to do. On the first day of every week, each one of you should set aside a sum of money in keeping with his income, saving it up, so that when I come no collections will have to be made.

2 Corinthians 8:1-9

And now, brothers, we want you to know about the grace that God has given the Macedonian churches. Out of the most severe trial, their overflowing joy and their extreme poverty welled up in rich generosity. For I testify that they gave as much as they were able, and even beyond their ability. Entirely on their own, they urgently pleaded with us for the privilege of sharing in this service to the saints. And they did not do as we expected, but they gave themselves first to the Lord and then to us in keeping with God's will. So we urged Titus, since he had earlier made a beginning, to bring also to completion this act of grace on your part. But just as you excel in everything—in faith, in speech, in knowledge, in complete earnestness and in your love for us—see that you also excel in this grace of giving.

I am not commanding you, but I want to test the sincerity of your love by comparing it with the earnestness of others. For you know the grace of our Lord Jesus Christ, that though he was rich, yet for your sakes he became poor, so that you through his poverty might become rich.

Titus 3:14

Our people must learn to devote themselves to doing what is good, in order that they may provide for daily necessities and not live unproductive lives.

Isn't it a privilege to be a trusted manager for Almighty God? That's what you are. And God wants to empower you to become even more trustworthy. Step out in faith. God will meet you!

Let's Pray

Join with me in this prayer:

Dear God, when it comes to my giving, I don't want to be like flint or a sponge. Lord, help me become a honeycomb! Teach me to give without the fear of running out of Your supply. Build my character so that giving the firstfruits of all my income will become as natural to me as breathing. Your Kingdom and Your glory are what I want to live for! In view of a returning Savior, I pray in Jesus' name. Amen.

2 Corinthians 8:7

But just as you excel in everything—in faith, in speech, in knowledge, in complete earnestness and in your love for us—see that you also excel in this grace of giving.

In the next few pages you'll discover:

- ❖ It's vital to keep growing in your giving.
- ❖ God is at work today in the lives of those who take Him at His Word.
- ❖ God works through you—especially when you give in faith.

WORD FOUR:
I Will Help You Give
More Than You Can Imagine

Several years ago, after a lunch meeting, I sat in the car talking with one of my older Christian friends. As the conversation moved toward giving, this wise, godly brother made a surprising comment. He told me, "When my wife and I got married, I decided we should grow in our giving until we could give over 50 percent to the Lord." I'll admit I thought that was impossible, if not downright crazy! Then my friend said, "It took us a few years, but you know what? We made it!"

This man wasn't wealthy when he decided to put God first in his giving, either. As time went by, though, he received numerous promotions, which resulted in a prominent position with a major retailing firm. First, the Lord gave him the desire to be generous; then He gave him blessings to match.

We need to hear more stories of faithful devotion to God that will encourage us to stretch higher in our giving and trust Him to provide the harvest.

Setting a Faith Budget

Well-known author Henry Blackaby has greatly impacted my thinking and teaching on giving. The following story illustrates his insight:

> One year the people on our finance committee said, "You have taught us to walk by faith in every area

of the life of our church except in the budget." I asked them to explain. They said, "Well, when we set the budget, we set the budget on the basis of what we believe we can do. It does not reflect that we expect God to do anything."

"Hmmm," I said. "Then how do you feel we ought to set the budget?"

They said, "First, we ought to determine all that God wants to do through us. Second, we need to put down what that will cost. Then we need to divide the budget goal into three categories: (1) what we plan to do through our tithes; (2) what others have promised to do; and (3) what we must depend on God to do."

As a church, we prayed and decided God wanted us to use this approach to budgeting. We did not try to dream our own dreams for God. We had to be absolutely sure God was leading us to do the things we put in the budget. Then we listed what that would cost. We listed what we thought our people would give and what others had said they would give. The difference between what we could reasonably expect to receive and the total was what we would ask God to provide.

The big question was: What is our operating budget? Well, by faith we adopted the grand total as our operating budget. At this point, we reached a crisis of belief. Did we really believe that the God who led us to do these things also would provide the resources to bring them to pass? Anytime God leads you to do something that has God-sized dimensions, you will face a crisis of belief. When you face a crisis of belief, what you do next reveals what you really believe about God.

The budget of our church normally would have been $74,000. The budget we set was $164,000. We pledged to pray daily that God would meet our needs. Any money that came in that we did not anticipate we credited to God. At the end of the year, we had received $172,000. God taught our church a lesson in faith that radically changed us all."[3]

That story didn't just change the members of that church, it changed me, too! These people gave more than they imagined they could. They honestly, prayerfully, and sincerely sought the Lord's will, even though their decisions caused a "crisis of belief." They learned that they would have to trust God to provide an amount far beyond what their experiences told them was possible. Then they decided to trust God, and God didn't let them down.

Are you going through a personal crisis of belief with your finances? If so, this discomfort may be God's way of getting your attention. As you prepare to receive the harvest God has promised you, you'll have to come face to face with the obstacles blocking your faith. Just like the people in Blackaby's story, you can lean on God in prayer and follow through as He leads you.

Sow Faithfully

By now, I am certain you are familiar with the phrase, "You reap what you sow." This is God's Law of the Harvest. It is a powerful motivation for you to continue to trust God and give during both the financially lean times as well as times of great financial harvest. If you will decide that no matter what, you will continue to sow, then like the church members in Henry Blackaby's story, you will be amazed at what God will accomplish.

Wait Patiently

Perhaps you have been an obedient giver for some time, following the Lord from your heart and trusting Him to bless you as you tithed faithfully. It might be that this series has encouraged you and motivated you to begin giving a tenth of your income to accomplish Kingdom purposes. Either way, once you have taken this important step, you move into the Faith Zone. The Faith Zone is the time between when you sow and when you reap. When you sow, you expect to reap, right? But no one expects to reap right away! It will take time before the harvest comes. But when we have faith in the process of sowing and reaping, we wait patiently. This means that time is the evidence of faith. The more time you wait, the greater the demonstration of your faith, as with Abraham.

If you are having a difficult time waiting for a financial breakthrough, think about the life of Abraham. This must be one of the most amazing stories of faith in the history of the world. God not only promised to give him a son, He promised to make from his offspring a complete nation. God waited until Abraham was a hundred years old and his wife Sarah was ninety years old—well past the age of childbearing. This promise would require nothing short of a miracle! But, as God said in Genesis 18:14, "Is anything too hard for the Lord?"

May I ask you the same question? Romans 4:16 tells us a principle that Abraham lived. The Bible says, "The promise comes by faith...." Abraham had to wait a long, long time before he saw the gift God had planned for him. But the time he waited not only allowed him to receive the promised blessing, it now serves as an irrefutable reminder to trust in God to provide for us and to use the resources we give back to Him to make an eternal impact. So keep believing!

Enjoy Your Blessings

To better enjoy what you have right now, think back on earlier days in your life when times were tight. For example, one of my favorite "early marriage contentment stories" takes me back to Tuesday nights. My wife and I lived in a little town where a local cinema charged only $1 a ticket each Tuesday. Also, on that same day the local pizza place had a "Two for One" coupon in the paper. So, on Tuesday evenings we often enjoyed pizza and a movie together for less than $10. Back then we didn't even realize that we were poor, because we had each other and we had the Lord. Experiencing God through the "lean times" creates a close bond with our Heavenly Father, and once the difficulties pass, we know He has been with us all the way. As the old gospel song goes, "Count your blessings, name them one by one, and it will surprise you what the Lord has done."

We really are more blessed here in the United States than we often realize. From my work around the world as a minister and missionary, I have witnessed many different cultures and socioeconomic situations. Each experience has taught me to be more appreciative of my current situation. In fact, as you count your blessings, don't forget to thank God that you can stand under hot water and take a shower in the morning. What a luxury!

The teaching and encouragement in this book is aimed at one central truth: You can trust God's Word. When the Lord of the universe promises us anything, have no fear or doubt that His Word will come to pass.

It is crucial for us to implant the truths of God's great promises of provision firmly into our minds and hearts. When they are, Satan will be disarmed. Both disobedience and fear, two of his most frequently used weapons, will lose their impact, and the work of expanding the Kingdom of Jesus will surge forward.

We must act in faith first and then expect God to honor His Word. It is similar to the example recorded in 2 Kings 3:9-20. The armies of Israel, Judah, and Edom were allied together in battle with the nation of Moab. During the course of one of their marches to engage the Moabites, the armies ran out of water for the men and their pack animals. The three kings met together to consider their options. King Jehoshaphat led the other two kings to visit the prophet Elisha and ask him for counsel from the Lord. Elisha responded, "This is what the LORD says: You will see neither wind nor rain, yet this valley will be filled with water, and you, your cattle and your other animals will drink. This is an easy thing in the eyes of the LORD; he will also hand Moab over to you" (vv. 17,18).

The armies followed Elisha's unusual instructions from God. They dug dry ditches and waited for God to fill them miraculously with water. The story continues, "The next morning, about the time for offering the sacrifice, there it was—water flowing from the direction of Edom! And the land was filled with water" (v. 20). Notice their faith in God to do something beyond their normal experience. Notice also the importance of the number of ditches they dug. Evidently, they dug lots of ditches because the land was "filled with water." The Lord had promised to fill every ditch they chose to dig, and He kept His promise.

What do you think would have happened if they had dug only a few ditches? Clearly, the Lord would have filled them, but the people would have missed the full blessing God intended. Do you see the point? When God tells us to be generous (1 Timothy 6:18) or to excel in the grace of giving (2 Corinthians 8:7), He is actually giving us an opportunity to "dig ditches" for Him to fill today. How many ditches are you digging? Your answer is evidence of how much belief you have in Him to fulfill all His promises, whether spiritual, physical, or emotional.

Our role is to follow Jesus, just like Peter did in Luke 5. Peter and his fishing partners had fished all night and failed to catch anything. After Jesus finished a morning of teaching, he told them to head back out into the deep water, drop their nets again, and expect a catch. Peter's conventional wisdom told him that going out again would be a waste of time. After all, they were experienced fishermen who had worked hard all night and failed to catch even a single fish! But his respect for Jesus caused him to consent. He told the Lord, "Because you say so, I will let down the nets" (Luke 5:5). The men pulled in a haul of fish so large their nets began to break! All this occurred because Peter took the Lord at His Word. When God makes a promise, He always comes through—often in remarkable ways.

Here's the bottom line: God is in the people business. More than anything He wants us to become like His Son, Jesus. To do this He will love us, bless us, discipline us, and develop us by the power of His Holy Spirit so that we become all He wants us to be. After all, this is entirely for our own good.

So experience the joy of generosity. Practice growing in the power of giving. Take God at His Word. You will experience the power of giving.

Think It Through

Word Four: I Will Help You Give More Than You Can Imagine

1. Imagine yourself as a member of the congregation in Henry Blackaby's story. Would your response to the committee's decision create a "crisis of belief" for you? Why?

2. What personal crisis of belief are you experiencing today? Pray for God's guidance to handle it.

3. Identify at least four attitudes about giving that God wants you to change. Pray about any barriers preventing your changes.

Meditate on God's Word

2 Corinthians 8:9-11

For you know the grace of our Lord Jesus Christ, that though he was rich, yet for your sakes he became poor, so that you through his poverty might become rich.

And here is my advice about what is best for you in this matter: Last year you were the first not only to give but also to have the desire to do so. Now finish the work, so that your eager willingness to do it may be matched by your completion of it, according to your means.

2 Corinthians 9:6,7

Remember this: Whoever sows sparingly will also reap sparingly, and whoever sows generously will also reap generously.

Each man should give what he has decided in his heart to give, not reluctantly or under compulsion, for God loves a cheerful giver.

Galatians 6:9,10

Let us not become weary in doing good, for at the proper time we will reap a harvest if we do not give up. Therefore, as we have opportunity, let us do good to all people, especially to those who belong to the family of believers.

Ephesians 3:20,21

Now to him who is able to do immeasurably more than all we ask or imagine, according to his power that is at work within us, to him be glory in the church and in Christ Jesus throughout all generations, for ever and ever! Amen.

Hebrews 11:6

And without faith it is impossible to please God, because anyone who comes to him must believe that he exists and that he rewards those who earnestly seek him.

How deeply do you desire the rewards God gives to His faithful, generous followers? Will you accept the challenge the Lord has laid on your heart?

Let's Pray...

Join me in prayer:

Heavenly Father, I sense these lessons have provided me with a fresh awareness of blessings from Your hand. Now it's time for me to take a step up in my willingness to take You at Your Word. Please grant me the grace to stand in the riches of Your provision and stretch to become like Your Son. I realize He became poor for my sake, and I have access to all Your riches. What a precious reality! I will praise You and thank You forever! By Jesus' power and love, I pray. Amen.

Endnotes

[1]Adapted from *God is Able* by Elmer Towns and John Maxwell (Lynchburg, VA: Church Growth Institute, 1986). Used by permission.

[2]John T. Willis, Ph.D., "Tithing and Other Kinds of Giving in the Old Testament." Used by permission.

[3]Henry Blackaby and Clyde King, *Experiencing God: Knowing and Doing the Will of God.* (Nashville: Lifeway Press, 1990), p. 108. All rights reserved. Used by permission.

About the Author

Dr. Kregg Hood is a national leader in stewardship-related ministry efforts that help churches and Christians give, save, spend, and invest their financial resources. His books and teaching programs on tithing and Christian financial wisdom have been used in more than 3,500 churches across the country.

Dr. Hood earned his doctorate in instructional communication from Texas Tech University. He also holds masters degrees in both missions and preaching. His undergraduate degree included majors in Bible, biblical languages, and mathematics.

Dr. Hood's personal ministry focus revolves around positive, practical preaching as well as teaching and writing on stewardship. He shares, "God's people are poised to really experience the impact of biblical and Holy Spirit-empowered truth about money. Our world needs God's wisdom as never before, and as we learn to better model the Lord's plan, we will be salt and light to millions. God is always on our side and He will always bless us when we trust Him and His promises."

Dr. Hood also serves as an adjunct professor at Evangel University, where he teaches a graduate course in Marketing and Public Relations. He is also a frequent guest preacher in churches around the country and a contributor to a wide variety of Christian magazines and newsletters.

Dr. Hood and his family make their home near Springfield, Missouri.